# When You Lose Someone You Love

*"Let the little children to come to me,
and do not hinder them,
for the kingdom of God belongs
to such as these."*

MARK 10:14

## Walter Albritton

*Walter Albritton*

# When You Lose Someone You Love

*Knowing God hurts like you hurt
helps you process the distressing grief
of losing a loved one*

*When You Lose Someone You Love*
Copyright © 2017
by Walter Albritton

All rights reserved. No part of this publication may be reproduced, stored in a retrieval system, or transmitted in any form or by any means, electronic, mechanical, photocopying, recording, or otherwise, without the prior permission of the author.

Scripture quotations, unless otherwise indicated, are from The Holy Bible, New International Version, NIV, used by permission of Zondervan.

This book was first published in 2011 with the title 233 Days. It has been revised, enlarged and reformatted.

Printed in the United States of America

Book Design: Susan Heslup

ISBN-13: 978-1979877756
ISBN-10: 1979877750

**Other books by Walter Albritton**

*If You Want to Walk On Water,
You've Got to Get Out of Your Boat*

*God Is Not Done with You*

*When Your Heart is Broken*

*The Great Secret*

*233 Days*

*Leaning Over the Banisters of Heaven*

*Life is Short So Laugh Often, Live Fully and Love Deeply*

*Just Get Over It and Move On!*

*Don't Let Go of the Rope!*

*Do the Best You Can with What You've Got,
Where You Are, While There's Time*

*You Simply Can't Trust a Talking Bird*

*The Four Gospels (Commentary on Selected Passages)*

*Paul's Letters (Commentary on Selected Passages)*

*Beacons of Hope
(Commentary on Selected New Testament Passages)*

Available from bookstores
or
walteralbritton7@gmail.com

**Dedicated to**

***Nels F. S. Ferre***

1908 – 1971

The teacher who introduced me
to the God who suffers

and to

The fellow strugglers whose faith inspired me to trust
the God who hurts like we hurt when we are walking
through the valley of the shadow of death

and

In Memory of

***David Walter Albritton***

April 18, 1953 – May 17, 1956

David Walter Albritton

## Moment of Truth

It was a grey and foggy morn
The day our son was born.
His presence made a brighter day
In a strange mysterious way.
Was it his radiant face,
Or his sweet embrace
That made us love him so?
I'm sure I'll never know.
But this much I know for sure
Our love was made to endure.

It was a day at its best
The morning we laid him to rest
How could the sun seem so bright
With our son no longer in sight?
Ashes to ashes and dust to dust,
Oh Lord, where do I put my trust?
Can there be another land
That is under your command?
My heart tells me it's true
For those who believe in you.

-- Dean Albritton

# CONTENTS

Preface ................................................................ xi
Introduction ........................................................ xii

Chapter 1    Born During a Storm ................................. 19

Chapter 2    Diagnosed with Leukemia ......................... 23

Chapter 3    The Numbness of Anticipating Death ...... 28

Chapter 4    Memories Became Precious ...................... 32

Chapter 5    Fun Playing in the Parks ........................... 36

Chapter 6    The Fraternity of Suffering ....................... 39

Chapter 7    "I love you Daddy" .................................... 43

Chapter 8    Praying Earnestly but Differently .............. 47

Chapter 9    The Kind Professor Playing with David ... 50

Chapter 10   Drinking Joy from Deathless Springs ....... 55

Chapter 11   Days of Mourning ...................................... 59

Chapter 12   Embracing Winning Attitudes ................... 66

## *Preface*

I am so glad Walter wrote the story of our son's suffering and death. Hundreds of people have shared with us how much David's story has helped them to cope with the suffering and death of a loved one. If, as you begin reading this book, you are struggling with grief, I believe you will find comfort and hope as Walter shares his heart with you.

It is fitting that David's father tells this story. Walter held David before I did on the first day of his life and David died in his father's arms when he breathed his last breath. Walter's love for David was steadfast and beautiful. And he has given to me and our four sons, who were gifts of God after David died, that same kind of steadfast love.

This story is worth telling because it changed our lives. Your life could be changed by this story. And if the telling of David's journey can help one person refuse to drink from the cup of bitterness, it will be worth all the pain we have relived.

The joy of arriving in heaven, for me, will be to see Walter holding David again. My faith clings to the belief that one day we will be together again. I can hear David say to Walter, "Dad, the man who lifted me up into the arms of Jesus on that last day of my life is here; you must come and thank him." I can close my eyes and still feel Nels Ferre holding us in his strong loving arms, faith radiating from his piercing blue eyes, and sharing transforming words of hope that gave us a reason to trust the God who was hurting like we were hurting.

My prayer, as you travel on the journey of grief, is that someone will love you into the transforming awareness that the God who feels your pain will soon turn your despair into joy. I know He can do it because He did it for me.

- Dean Albritton

## *Introduction*

"Your son is going to die. There is no cure for this type of leukemia. All we can do is make him comfortable until the end." Those were the most shocking words I had ever heard. Our son, our only child, was dying and there was nothing we could do about it. It was the most helpless moment of my life.

Had the subject of grief come up at that time in my life, I would have agreed that life is about birth and death. Birth is about pain and joy. Death is about pain and sorrow. But I would have assumed death was in the distant future. Suddenly, without warning, death was in my lap. And I was not prepared to cope with it.

Someone I loved was about to be taken from me. Death is about loss. Loss is about pain, excruciating pain when the one you are losing is someone whose life you have treasured. I had no idea how paralyzing sorrow would be or how agonizing the grief process would be.

You may have had a similar experience. You may be reading this book because grief has suddenly come upon you like a whirlwind. The advice of your friends has not released you from the numbing stranglehold of grief. The strange ideas of some people ("God needed another angel in heaven") have angered more than comforted you. And the God questions torment you. How can you believe that God loves you when he allows someone you love to suffer and die?

You may be on the brink, as I once was, of drinking from the fountain of bitterness. I had the cup to my lips. But that is why I have written this story, the story not only of our son's suffering and death but of my journey from doubting God's love to the confidence that God hurts like we hurt when grief has us by the throat.

Having been a pastor most of my life, I have watched many people die. Some were at peace. Some were not. What is the difference? The difference is peace with God. The only way to "be at peace" is to have peace with God.

Things cannot provide the peace we need in our souls. Peace with God cannot be achieved; it can only be received since it is a gift, and God alone is the giver. He gives the gift of peace to those who desire, above all else, to live in harmony with God.

This is where the soul comes in. Harmony comes through getting the soul grounded in God. Harmony with God never comes until we decide that pleasing God is more important than pleasing ourselves with the things of this world.

In one of his books Dallas Willard explains it this way: "Our soul is like a stream of water, which gives strength, direction and harmony to every other area of our life. When that stream is as it should be, we are constantly refreshed and exuberant in all we do, because our soul itself is then profusely rooted in the vastness of God and his kingdom, including nature; and all else within us is enlivened and directed by that stream. Therefore, we are in harmony with God, reality, and the rest of human nature and nature at large."

Harmony happens when attitudes change. I have little harmony with God when I am focused on being recognized and applauded for my achievements. Harmony comes when I choose to put other people first and give up seeking the applause of others.

Dallas Willard explains how this works: "If you want to really experience the flow of love as never before, the next time you are in a competitive situation (around work or relationship or whose kids are the highest achieving or looks or whatever), pray that the others around you will be more outstanding, more praised, and more used of God than yourself. Really pull for them and rejoice in their success. If Christians were universally to do this for each other, the earth would soon be filled with the knowledge of the glory of God."

Think about the options we have. If I get passed over for a promotion, I can moan and groan about how I was mistreated. Or I can thank God for what I do have and help celebrate the good fortune of the person who got the promotion. I have no peace as long as what matters is my own achievements and material wealth.

Horatio Spafford lost everything in the Great Chicago Fire of 1871. He lost his money and his home. He had no insurance. A short time after that his four daughters were drowned in a shipwreck. Despite his losses, Spafford had harmony with God. Otherwise he could not have written this testimony of faith in the hymn he composed:

*When peace, like a river, attendeth my way,*
*When sorrows like sea billows roll;*
*Whatever my lot, Thou hast taught me to say,*
*It is well, it is well with my soul.*

In the New Testament the Apostle Peter says that the salvation of our souls is "the end result" of our faith. Dallas Willard reminds us that "The salvation of your soul is not just about where you go when you die. The word salvation means healing or deliverance at the deepest level of who we are in the care of God through the presence of Jesus. Sooner or later, your world will fall apart. What will matter then is the soul you have constructed."

I have learned to think of problems as opportunities though I must admit it is extremely difficult to look upon the death of a loved one as an opportunity. But actually, it is. Even when I am depressed, heartbroken and fighting back tears, I can be kind to the people around me, especially those who are trying to help or comfort me. In my brokenness I need help, but my caregivers, my family and friends, need help also. My kindness helps them to feel they are making a difference.

There are few things in this world finer than kindness. To be treated with indifference is demeaning; it makes you sicker. To be treated with kindness helps you feel a sense of worth without which wellness is devoid of meaning.

Grief, like pain and illness, can produce fear and fill the mind with wretched thoughts. At my age every serious illness causes me to wonder if the end is near. I know it will come one day. Have I looked upon the faces of my loved ones for the last time? Is the time of my departure at hand? Scripture helps us overcome fear. It did for me one morning when my friend Ed Williams posted this on Facebook:

*I lie down and sleep; I wake again,*
*because the Lord sustains me.*
*I will not fear though tens of thousands*
*assail me on every side.*
Psalms 3:5-6

The liberating four words that chased away my fear – "I will not fear." That affirmation became the wind under my wings that day. Senseless fears were cast aside for I realized I was in touch with someone who will sustain me to the end of this journey called life.

Not long ago a highly contagious illness made it necessary for me to be isolated for two weeks. I consoled myself by remembering that I was not the first person to be quarantined. I have known others who spent greater time in isolation.

Saint Paul wrote some of his New Testament letters while holed up in a stinking prison. John Bunyan wrote Pilgrim's Progress during his long imprisonment. And not so long ago Martin Luther King Jr composed some famous letters from a Birmingham jail.

My confinement gave me the opportunity to study the paintings on the wall in my room. When we are busy with the affairs of life we only glance at wall paintings. For several days I gazed at some paintings with profit to my soul.

The most delightful painting in my room was titled "Dance of Grace." A smiling Jesus is dancing in a circle with several children and you can almost hear the music to which they were dancing. I went online and discovered that Mark Keathley did not intend for his painting to illustrate a moment in the life of Jesus but to depict the delight and celebration that Jesus invites everyone to join in the present. I got up with my walking stick and danced around the room for a few minutes. A fun moment interrupted the monotony of isolation.

Another large painting that hangs over the head of my bed is precious to my wife and to me. The painter used a palette knife and striking colors to portray a spectacular arrangement of peonies. She bought it "on time" when we were young and had hardly enough money to buy groceries. After paying ten dollars a month for almost a year, she brought it home and sheepishly admitted how she had obtained it. "Once I saw it, I had to have it," she said.

If our house catches on fire, I know Dean will haul that painting out first and then coming looking for me. I love the painting not only for its beauty; I cherish it because it reminds me that I am married to a woman who knows the meaning of sacrifice. She was willing to eat sardines and crackers in order to obtain something that has beautified every home we have lived in. But I still don't care for sardines. They make hamburger helper taste good.

I mention all this because the death of our son David changed everything for us. It changed the way we thought about living and dying. It changed our attitude toward things. It changed the way we looked at food, flowers, birds, grass and trees. It changed we way we thought about people and the way we looked at ourselves. Most of all, it changed the way we felt about God.

Until David was diagnosed with leukemia Dean and I had a casual attitude toward God. God was to us a great God – Creator, Redeemer, Sustainer, Provider and Savior of the world. <u>Our faith was quite orthodox but untested</u>. We were both raised in the church, Dean in the Baptist Church and I in the Methodist.

We had been taught in Sunday School that Jesus was our Friend, the Good Shepherd, the Bread of Life, the Water of Life, the King of Kings and the Savior who had washed away our sins with his blood. But all of these ideas were beliefs to which we were not emotionally attached. We believed these biblical tenets with the same detachment that we believed water was wet and sugar was sweet.

Then all hell broke loose. We were rudely snatched from a life centered in pleasure to one centered in pain. Death left his calling card with a promise to come back soon and torture us with his foreboding presence. Without warning we became students in the School of Suffering.

We were crushed, angry, disillusioned, bewildered and broken. We were trapped in the dark tunnel of anguish and realized there was no way out. We felt helpless, afraid and alone. Our Sunday School God could not meet our need. We desperately needed a God who would come to our rescue but the One who healed the sick and caused the blind to see did not seem to answer when we called.

I pray this book will be for you more than the story of one couple's struggle with suffering, death, doubt, anger and grief. I hope it will help you walk through your own journey of grief and find hope and joy as you walk out of the darkness into God's light. Let God use your pain to transform your despair into joy. I know He can do it. He has done it for me.

Wade into these words. Walk with Dean and me through our pain and bewilderment. Then share with us the joy of discovering that God hurts when we suffer and wants to use our pain for our good and His glory.

To God be the glory!

Walter Albritton, sjc<br>Servant of Jesus Christ

The Cabin
Wetumpka, Alabama
Thanksgiving, 2017

# 1

## Born During a Storm

*One day after I had been weeks in pain,*
*my Christian mother overheard me praying,*
*"Dear Lord, if thou wilt ever have me well*
*and use me again,*
*thy will be done;*
*if not, thy will be done anyway."*
*"Nels," she reproved, "that's no way to pray.*
*Thank Him and praise Him;*
*thank Him and praise Him."*
*This I did;*
*then I better understood*
*what adoration meant.*
*God's will is constantly for the best,*
*whatever happens.*
*Come what may,*
*He is to be thanked and praised.*

- Nels F. S. Ferre

*The Lord is close to the brokenhearted and saves those*
*who are crushed in spirit. -- Psalm 34:18*

**DOCTOR THOMAS SMILED AS HE WALKED TOWARD ME IN THE HOSPITAL WAITING ROOM.** "You have a fine baby boy," he said, beaming. He assured me both my son and his mother were just fine.

I have a son and his name will be David! Breathing a sigh of relief I hurried down the hall to check on my wife. We had not known the sex of our baby. We had decided if it was a boy we would name him David Walter after his grandfathers and that we did.

David was a beautiful baby. I will admit it - I counted his fingers and his toes! He had the right number. I was nervous, afraid at first that I might hurt him or drop him. He relaxed in my arms. I looked at Dean and smiled, thinking, "You have given me a precious son!"

Family and friends agreed that our first child was a prize specimen. His blue eyes and blond hair prompted friends to chuckle and ask, "Who is the father?" Neither Dean nor I was blessed with either of those features. We would smile and hope they believed our explanation – those genes came from my father. He did have blond hair and piercing blue eyes.

David was the center of our lives. He was born in April, less than a year after our June marriage. We were childhood sweethearts but waited until we were 20 to tie the knot. Our parents were relieved when we finally married. We actually met in the first grade and grew up together in the little town of Wetumpka, Alabama. Dean lived in town and I lived in the country. Our families did not get acquainted until we became teenagers.

Dean and I began married life in an upstairs garage apartment on College Street across from Auburn United Methodist Church. Dean was soon pregnant. After she fell down the stairs leading to our apartment we rented a house on Lakeview Drive in Auburn. The rent was a whopping $75 per month. I was in my third year at API (Alabama Polytechnic Institute), the land-grant college that would soon become known as Auburn University.

Early on the morning of April 18 we hurried off to the small Opelika hospital that is now called East Alabama Medical Center. Dean's sharp and increasingly rapid labor pains convinced her that today she would deliver her firstborn. Dark clouds and the forecast of bad weather made us a little uneasy. But it was the turbulence of childbirth not the weather that got our attention that day.

The raging storm forced the hospital to switch to emergency power when nearby power lines went down. Rain was hitting the windows in torrents. Water even poured into the hospital through the air-conditioning ducts. But we were safe inside, unaware that a tornado had ripped through the community. Our only concern was the delivery of our first child.

Our kind physician, Dr. Ben Thomas, had to drive from Auburn through a torrential rainstorm get to the hospital. Shortly after his arrival, debris from the storm made driving in the area quite hazardous.

When I returned home that night, elated by the safe delivery of our first son, I found our house had been damaged by the storm. The roof had been ripped off above the front door, allowing the rain to soak some of our furniture. But the damage seemed incidental compared to the total destruction of several nearby homes.

Weighing nine pounds and two ounces, our baby boy was handsome and healthy. His mom had survived the pain and fear of giving birth to her first child. We had started our family. We loved each other and life was good. That we had very little money did not worry us. We would work hard and together we would make it.

# 2

# Diagnosed with Leukemia

*What the bereaved man needs
is not the comfort of some
platitudes about death;
what he needs is a living faith
in the Living God,
and then he can comfort himself.*

- Elton Trueblood

*Though you have made me see troubles, many and bitter,
you will restore my life again; from the depths of the earth
you will again bring me up. -- Psalm 71:20*

**DAVID WAS 14 MONTHS OLD WHEN I GOT MY CAP AND GOWN AND RECEIVED MY B.S. DEGREE FROM AUBURN.** Six months later during Christmastime we moved to Nashville, Tennessee. To prepare for the ordained ministry I had enrolled in the Divinity School of Vanderbilt University. Having no money for a moving van we moved ourselves to Nashville in a borrowed truck. Once the tuition for school was paid we had only a few dollars left for living expenses. Like it or not we both had to work to survive and David was only 20 months old.

Dean found a job as the secretary of a Methodist Church. I got a part-time job with the Methodist Publishing House. With both of us working David would have to stay in a day care center. He fiercely resisted the idea and that disturbed deeply Dean and me. But despite the gut-wrenching agony of listening to him scream as we drove away, we felt we had no choice. Later we would regret that decision as much as any we ever made. Home, however humble, is the best place for an infant. Sadly, we realized that too late. But that is water over the dam.

By September that year I was deeply immersed in my seminary studies, attending classes in the morning and working into the night to make ends meet. David was two and though life was hard we were happy and completely unaware that our world was about to be turned upside down.

In early September David became ill. Nothing serious we

thought – a rash, fever or simply a bad cold. Dean took him to our pediatrician, Dr. T. Forte Bridges. His diagnosis was chickenpox, a common childhood disease. When the usual remedies for chickenpox had not worked, Dean took David back to see the good doctor. The medicine he had prescribed seemed to have no effect on David's low-grade fever.

Suspecting leukemia, Doctor Bridges told us he wanted to test the bone marrow by extracting a sample from David's breastbone or sternum. Children with acute leukemia will have too many white blood cells and not enough red blood cells or platelets. Many of the white blood cells in the blood will be "blasts," an early type of blood cell normally found only in the bone marrow. We agreed to the test and waited fearfully for the results.

On the last Tuesday in September Doctor Bridges called and asked both of us to come in for a meeting with him. We were puzzled but little suspected that this conference with the doctor would become the worst day of our lives.

Our appointment was at 2 pm on Tuesday, September 28. Arriving early we were ushered into a conference room and asked to sit together on one side of a large oak table. Soon Doctor Bridges walked in, faintly smiling but grim-faced. He got right to the point. "I am afraid I have bad news for you. The bone marrow test confirmed my suspicion. David has acute lymphocytic leukemia."

Leukemia! I did not even know how to spell the word. We sat there in shock, speechless and terrified. Slowly it began to sink in; David had a problem the doctor could not fix. There was no cure for leukemia. Trembling and afraid I finally asked the doctor to explain what we faced. His words burned their way into my brain as he began telling us about this dreadful disease that is the most common form of cancer in children. (It is also known as acute lymphoblastic leukemia.)

"Leukemia," he explained, "is a form of cancer, a cancer of blood-forming cells in the bone marrow. It causes immature cells to accumulate in the blood and within organs of the body. They are not able to carry out the normal functions of blood cells."

Normal blood, he told us, contains three groups of cells: white blood cells, red blood cells, and platelets. "Lymphocytic" refers to the white blood cells, called lymphocytes, which this type of leukemia affects.

"Acute" means that the disease progresses rapidly and the doctor said sadly, "There is nothing we can do to stop it. All we can do is to try to make David as comfortable as possible until the end."

After a long pause, my vision blurred by tears, I asked the inevitable question: "How long does he have?" With obvious compassion the doctor said quietly, "I don't really know. I would guess that he has from two months to possibly two years." His answer sent a chill up and down my spine. I could hardly breathe.

Almost as an afterthought the kind doctor offered us a thread of hope. There is always, he said, the possibility that researchers will discover a cure in time. He explained that a lot of research was going on. Eventually the research did pay off but not in time to help our David. Nowadays the diagnosis of leukemia is not a death sentence for a child.

In fact a few years ago our great granddaughter, Zoey Albritton, was treated for leukemia and later declared free of the dread disease. We rejoice in the progress medical science has made in curing leukemia victims.

Our visit with the doctor lasted only a few minutes. He had others who needed his attention. The pain of this dreadful news did last – into a sleepless night and into months of groping for answers and struggling with the question of how to make David's final days meaningful.

Blinded by tears we stumbled out of Baptist Hospital, hardly able to find our car in the parking lot. I remember standing on the lawn, frozen in time and feeling like a basket case, aimlessly watching people walking on the sidewalks while traffic moved up and down the streets as usual. Reality hit me like a sledgehammer blow between my eyes – life goes on! Traffic does not stop to recognize your pain. People go on about their business. If you stop to lament your misfortune you will get run over in the street. You are not the first person to suffer. So handle your pain. Dry your tears and cope with it. The world will not stop so you can get off the merry-go-round.

# 3

## The Numbness of Anticipating Death

*It is very important
that we never conclude
that only the pleasant and the beautiful
have positive value.
The truth of the matter is
that life is a bittersweet reality,
and that is its essence and its glory.
For the final outcome
both the sunshine
and the shadows are needed.*

- John Claypool

*My heart is in anguish within me; the terrors of death assail me.
Fear and trembling have beset me; horror has overwhelmed me.
-- Psalm 55:4-5*

**Bewildered by leukemia's invasion into our lives, we did our best to suck it up and play the hand we had been dealt.** Our life had to go on too. There were bills to pay, even more now with all the medicine and medical attention David needed. While our friends expressed their concern for us, we were left to resume the customary routines of daily life.

The stunning awareness that our son was going to die changed abruptly our attitude about life. When we were children our big concern was to have fun, enjoy life and play games. We never worried about paying bills or the meaning of life, much less death. But reality has a rude way of interrupting fun and games so even children must wrestle with trouble. Eventually trouble finds us all.

My wife remembers a harsh, cold Christmas. Her daddy was dead. There was no money. Her mother said, without shedding a tear, "There will be no gifts this Christmas. We have food to eat. That is all there is." Life was not fun and games for my wife that Christmas. She was only seven years old but she had to find a way to face trouble and not allow it to ruin her life.

Growing up on a farm I learned that farming is hard work. There was little time for fun and games. My father worked from sunup until sundown and he tolerated nothing less from his farm hands and his children. He was tough as nails. Gentle he was not. But I loved him and respected him. He was a man's man.

Dad did allow me to have a dog. He was a Boxer and I called him Bull. For a few years that dog provided incredible meaning to my life. We were inseparable though he was a yard dog. I was grown before I heard the word "pedigree." Neither dogs nor cats were allowed inside the house. I would think it strange later to find that some of my friends slept with a dog or cat beside them in their bed.

Bull earned his keep. He learned how to help us drive cattle from one field to another. Cows paid attention to his barking. He could quickly turn a stray calf back to the herd.

With Bull beside me I had no fear when it was necessary to go searching in the woods for a tardy milk cow. Bull was my protection against whatever monsters might be lurking in the shadows. An angry snake or a snarling bobcat would be no match for Bull. Life was good in those days. I had read a book about Lassie and the boy who loved him. Bull was not as handsome as Lassie but he was my dog and I loved him.

It never occurred to me that Bull might die. Then tragedy struck. James Porterfield, Dad's right-hand man for managing the farm, was cutting hay. Bull was playing in the field near the tractor, chasing a rabbit now and then, just enjoying life. Suddenly James came running up, panic stricken, with Bull lying helpless in the back of the truck. The mower blade had cut off three of his legs.

Realizing how alarmed I was, my dad responded with unusual compassion. He must have known there was nothing the veterinarian could do for Bull. Nonetheless he yielded to my plea to "take Bull to the doctor so he could sew his legs back on." I had carefully wrapped the severed legs up in a rag, sure that the veterinarian could "fix" Bull.

The vet was a kind man. I could tell that he hurt with me. After examining Bull, however, he said sadly, "Son, there is no way for me to sew his legs back on. I am sorry but the only thing we can do is to put Bull to sleep." There was no funeral. We left my beloved Bull with the vet and drove back home, mostly in silence. Dad seemed to understand my grief.

The shock of that day is burned into my memory. Life would never be the same. Trouble had come and delivered a crushing blow to my heart. Somehow I found a way to embrace my dog's death but now, a decade later, I was facing the death of my own child, a far greater challenge. I was numb and devastated.

# 4

## Memories Became Precious

*The capacity to appreciate life*
*has something to do with*
*the capacity to deal with death.*
*Those who appreciate life*
*are better able to deal with death.*
*Those who do not value the gift of life*
*have greater trouble dealing with death.*
*Were it not for the gift of life,*
*we would not be alive*
*to worry about our death.*
*Give thanks to God for life.*
*Be at peace about death.*

- Kennon L. Callahan

*Hear my prayer, O Lord, listen to my cry for help;*
*be not deaf to my weeping. -- Psalm 39:12*

**I HAD SELDOM ENCOUNTERED DEATH.** No one in my immediate family had died. I did remember my cousin Buck Johnson dying when I was a teenager. Buck was riding in the back of a pick-up truck when a tire blew out. He was thrown off the truck and died instantly in a ditch. His sudden, senseless death was a terrible shock to his parents Seth and Kathleen Johnson. I remembered how they grieved and how their sorrow forever changed and aged them. Sudden death is so devastating. At least Dean and I had time to prepare for the death of our son. But I found little consolation in that.

If you are ever going to pray you will pray when death is staring you in the face. We did pray. But I confess I had my doubts about whether God was listening. Does it do any good to pray for the sick? Is God going to do what he does whether we pray or not? If God is going to do whatever he wishes to do, why bother praying at all? Why not relax, forget praying, and agree with those who believe that "whatever will be, will be"? I had more questions than answers.

But I prayed hard. I begged God to heal my son. I knew very little about prayer back then. I know a little more now but I am still learning. I have learned that one does not pray to change God's mind but to accept God's will. God is not a cosmic vendor who gives us what we ask for when we pray the right prayers. He is the Father who knows what is best for us, and whose will is for our good even when we do not understand what he is doing. I believe that now but when David was dying I did not understand that.

Some of life's best lessons are learned through pain. I read somewhere that "One can see farther through a tear than through a telescope." That was true for me. Through the tears I shed while David was dying I saw many things more clearly than ever before.

David was actually not terribly "sick" at first. His medicine soothed his fever and for awhile he was able to walk and play as usual. Then we noticed a gradual weakening of his strength. This continued slowly until he became bed-ridden and unable to walk. An invisible enemy was robbing him of his life.

Memories suddenly became precious to us. We recalled little things and silly things that had happened – like the first time David fell off the bed. He was hardly two months old and the sound of his hitting the floor scared us to death. He was not hurt but I figured his skull had been fractured or an arm had been broken.

We remembered the visits that friends and family members had made to see our son during his first year. We were loved. David was loved. Life was good. The thought of David dying never entered our minds.

Funny moments were recalled – like the one in church when David was five months old. I had begun serving as the pastor of four country churches. There we made some of the best friends we ever had. Frank Hugh and Louise Pearce were so special to us. (On the day David died Frank Hugh rented a station wagon; then he drove to Nashville with my dad to take David's body home to Wetumpka for the funeral. It was a priceless gift of love on Frank Hugh's part. He was not a wealthy man but he was rich toward God.)

Two of my churches expected the pastor's wife to play the piano during worship services. Dean agreed and did while I held David in my arms; like most infants he was not happy in the arms of strangers. One Sunday while I was praying, with my eyes closed as usual, David poked his hand into my mouth as though to say, "Stop praying such long prayers!"

We recalled the drought of David's second year. No rain fell for months and the ground was parched. My first garden was a disaster and the well at the parsonage went dry. We had to haul water to the house for several weeks. We boiled some of the water to be sure it was safe for our baby.

David began walking at ten months so he found his way into everything in our little parsonage. There was nothing he did not check out. Ink was everywhere after he examined the old mimeograph machine we used to make church bulletins. The machine was in my small office at home. David used some of the ink to make several interesting marks in one or two of my commentaries – marks that back then prompted anger but are treasures today.

# 5

# Fun Playing in the Parks

*God does not permit ~~pain~~ because of a delight in our suffering. God (personally) enters into our suffering and shares ~~it, the~~ incarnation makes God's participation abundantly clear.
So, in our suffering, we can count on the unseen presence of God to sustain us until we see clearly to discern God's will.*

- Ben Campbell Johnson

*But the Lord stood at my side and gave me strength.*
*-- 2 Timothy 4:17*

**AN INCURABLE ILLNESS ABRUPTLY CHANGES THE WAY YOU LIVE.** We had to have help. Our families were too far away to provide that help. If I stayed in school, working part-time, and Dean continued to work, we had to have someone in the house on a daily basis.

Four days after the diagnosis we found Winnie Pye. Winnie was a practical nurse and unemployed at the time. She quickly accepted our offer of a job. Winnie was a special gift of God and soon became dearer than life to the three of us. This allowed us both to continue working and me to continue my classes at Vanderbilt. Winnie came to our home every day to clean and cook and help us care for David. If ever anyone was on special assignment from God, it was Winnie Pye.

Two beautiful parks in Nashville were havens of blessing to us during the early months of David's illness. Centennial Park is the home of the famous replica of the Parthenon. We began visiting the Parthenon to enjoy its splendor and to learn more about ancient Greece. Later we visited for the comfort it brought to see something sturdy and unchanging.

The four bronze doors of this unique building weigh seven and a half tons each. They measure 24 feet high and seven feet wide, making them the largest set of matching bronze doors in the world. The magnificent park outside became a favorite place for picnics, playing on the grass and simply enjoying the manicured landscape, the beautiful flowers and the fountains in the ponds. David loved throwing bread to the ducks. We can still see him tossing bread to the hungry ducks.

Centennial Park was also special because of the train engine on the north side of the park. The huge engine was "David's train." Parked there for many years, the engine is a favorite for children because a child can climb up in the cab and wave as though he is the engineer. David never tired of going to see his train. We can still see him waving to us. Never doubt the wisdom of people who do strange things like parking a retired train engine in a park. That train was worth its weight in gold to us.

Percy Warner Park is a much larger park in which people can drive through lovely woods and fields and find picnic tables in many delightful locations. Many Saturdays and Sundays, with limited money for eating out, we found our way to Percy Warner. There we enjoyed many special times with David especially when family and friends came for a visit. We could throw some food in a basket, get out of the house and celebrate life with this special child who would soon slip away.

# The Fraternity of Suffering

*We are not living wisely or well
unless we recognize that
whatever we prize most
we hold by a slender thread
which may, at any moment,
be broken.*

- Elton Trueblood

*It was good for me to be afflicted so that I might learn your decrees.
-- Psalm 119:71*

**WE HAD DAVID FOR THREE CHRISTMASES.** The first was wonderful. David was eight months old. What fun we had with our firstborn! We had life by the tail; the future was ours.

The second Christmas was even better. David was 20 months old, walking and talking, able to enjoy family gatherings, good food, and the thrill of Santa Claus bringing gifts down the chimney.

Our final Christmas with David was bittersweet. It was good and it was horrible. Tears flowed freely in quiet places when no one was looking. The gaudy trappings of Christmas never seemed more irrelevant or more superficial. We longed for Christmas to come. Once it came we wanted even more for it to go away.

If Christmas is anything, it is a fun time for children but when a child is dying, the fun seems artificial, almost repugnant. After all a stocking filled with fruit, nuts and candy can bring precious little joy to a dying child. The loving support of family and friends helped us endure that Christmas.

Though David was too weak to walk, we still dressed him in his Cowboy suit and held him so he could ride the Rocking Horse Santa brought him. We could not afford it; we did it anyway. A little more debt was the least of our worries. We made lots of pictures that we still cherish though looking at them now stirs a mix of memories, most of which are tinged with sadness.

Before Christmas we had begun the awful routine of taking David to the hospital for blood transfusions. His doctor insisted the transfusions were necessary to keep David alive. Handling this was pure hell. Needless to say David never agreed to a single transfusion. I can still hear him begging me, "Please Daddy don't let them hurt me!"

Despite his tearful pleas, I helped the nurses hold David down so the blood transfusions could be completed. Transfusions take time; each one was hell for David as well as for me and his mother. To this day I am not sure I did the right thing. The transfusions only prolonged his life for a few months. I only know that at the time it seemed the right thing to do since it was the only way to keep David alive. I hope one day in heaven David will forgive me for allowing him to suffer pain that seemed unnecessary to him.

In the days of David's suffering we were in and out of Baptist Hospital many times. Dean and I were young and naïve. We had no idea most hospitals have a Children's Wing where many children are treated for various ailments. But there, in that wing, our eyes were opened. We discovered that we were not the only suffering parents. Some children were in worst condition than our David. Cancer wears many ugly faces. It dawned on us that there is a Fraternity of Suffering and we had become members. Painfully we offered each other what sympathy and comfort we could muster.

We also learned the sad story of the illness and death of a professor of medicine at Vanderbilt University. At age 46 Dr. David Rabin was diagnosed with Lou Gehrig's disease. He battled the muscular disease for four years and died at age 50. During those four years he grew weaker, gradually losing control of every muscle in his body except one - his eyebrow. He found a computer that could be controlled by the twitch of his eyebrow.

Amazingly David Rabin used this one remaining muscle to run his computer. Somehow he was able to write papers, speak to his family, and carry on a medical consulting practice. During his suffering he even published a textbook on endocrinology and won recognition for his work.

Hearing about Rabin's struggle at the time we were trying to cope with David's affliction made me keenly aware that <u>to be a human being is to suffer. Suffering is a universal reality.</u> But Rabin's courage impacted my thinking. I saw something I had never seen before. Though suffering is inevitable, it is possible to face it with such courage that fellow sufferers are inspired to endure their anguish with some degree of dignity and hope. So I prayed for the courage to bear our suffering without caving in to the despair and self-pity that constantly threatened to suffocate us.

After Christmas our constant load of pain and frustration became even heavier. The transfusions were more frequent; the effect was less and less helpful. Slowly the number of red blood cells was diminishing as the malignant white blood cells continuously multiplied. The eventual result, without life-giving red blood cells, would be death. The white blood cells were winning the war in his veins.

# 7

## "I love you Daddy"

*The more we know and love God*
*the more we ought to practice wordless prayers.*
*In the deepest moments of their lives*
*men are struck dumb and numb*
*not only with sorrow*
*but with deep joy.*

- Nels F. S. Ferre

*Then they cried to the Lord in their trouble, and he saved them from their distress. He brought them out of darkness and the deepest gloom and broke away their chains. -- Psalm 107:13-14*

**BY APRIL THE QUESTION WAS NOT IF DAVID WOULD DIE BUT WHEN.** During that terrible spring every time the phone rang I expected it to be Dean calling to ask me to come home quickly. That made for miserable days at work and at school. We lived under the constant dread that the end was near but it was all out of our control. Helpless does not begin to describe how we felt in those weeks.

Since David could not walk we secured a wheelchair but David hated it. He refused every request to get in it. One sunny day in February Dean decided it would be good to get out of the house. She dressed David warmly and forced him to sit in the wheelchair. Thinking he might enjoy a change of scenery Dean began pushing him along the sidewalk. Angrily David kept muttering, "I want to go home." Dean had no choice but to give up and take him back inside, her heart broken by David's stubbornness.

David's attitude added to the misery of those months. We were already dying inside, unable to alleviate David's suffering. But his disposition at times was almost unbearable. We blamed it on the medicine; perhaps it was both the disease and the medicine. Whatever the reason, David frequently rebuffed our kindness as though he was a grumpy old man.

One example will suffice. Late one afternoon I arrived home from work just as Dean was bringing David's supper to his bed. I watched as she propped him up with pillows and then placed a tray of his favorite food before him.

With one hand he swatted the tray into the floor; the milk and the food splattered everywhere.

At this point discipline was out of the question. Dean was speechless; she began to cry softly. I rebuked him mildly, having no idea why he would do such a thing. We cleaned the floor as David sat stewing in obvious frustration and embarrassment.

On impulse I decided to pick David up and take him for a walk up the street, giving Dean a few minutes to recover from this painful scene. David's stubbornness continued. "Let me alone," he said; "I don't want to go anywhere!"

Determined, I held him tightly in my arms and started walking up the sidewalk, only to discover that it was misting rain. I covered his head and walked on. He continued to struggle, hitting me with his fists. I tightened my hold on him and walked on, rain or no rain. I said nothing but silently I was praying, "Oh God, why are you letting this happen to us? Why?" I heard no answer.

After a few minutes David relaxed in my arms. Then he raised the little fists that he had been hitting me with and put his arms around my neck. His head was snuggled up against my chest and under my chin. To my astonishment he began talking. "Daddy, I'm sorry; I'm sorry. I didn't mean to do it. I'm sorry."

Tears streamed down my checks, mingling with the light rain, as I spoke gently to David, "It's alright Son; it's alright. I understand."

He replied, "I love you Daddy; I love you."

My voice cracked as I squeezed him and responded, "I love you too, Son."

The rain was coming down harder so I hurried back to the house, eager to share what had happened with Dean. I did not know it then but in years to come I would remember that walk in the rain as one of the most precious experiences of our journey through hell with our son.

David was potty-trained early and seldom wet his pants after his first year. That all changed as leukemia ravaged his body. One morning during his final months we found that he had wet the bed during the night. When Dean tried to move him so she could change the sheets, he screamed, "Don't touch me! Don't touch me!" His pain was so excruciating that he begged us not to move him. We had no choice but to wait awhile. It was an hour or so later before we could get him in some dry clothes.

# Praying Earnestly but Differently

*I can think of no place I want to be known so well
as on my knees,
confessing my own sins and faults
and finding the strength and forgiveness
to start again.*

- Nels F. S. Ferre

*I have told you these things so that in me you may have peace.
In this world you will have trouble. But take heart!
I have overcome the world. -- John 16:33*

**DURING DAVID'S ILLNESS WE RECEIVED A LOT OF ADVICE.** Some told us that if we had enough faith God would hear our prayers and heal David. In retrospect I guess we did not have enough faith. One person told us about a preacher in Texas whose prayers were healing the sick. He said, "Take David to Texas and let that man pray for him." Someone else told us to take David to Oklahoma and ask another evangelist to pray for his healing. We discussed the matter and decided that if God wanted to heal David, he could heal him in Tennessee as easily as Texas or Oklahoma.

We did invite people to pray for David's healing. Many people wrote us caring letters and assured us that they were praying for a miracle. We realized that only a miracle of God could save David from this incurable disease.

Some friends tried to prepare us for the grief we would face. We learned about the "stages" of grief – shock and denial, anger and bargaining, guilt and blame, acceptance and hope. Years passed before we began to understand grief. But the slight understanding we gained from caring friends helped us get through those stages. We tried to bargain with God; we asked him to let us die in David's place. But we soon realized that God was not going to accept our offer.

Dean and I prayed much – dare I say constantly? – during those agonizing 233 days between the diagnosis in September and David's death in May. But our prayers were different. She prayed the submissive prayer of a tough realist, asking God to give us strength to accept the inevitable and to stand up under the strain. She prayed for grace. I prayed for a miracle. I prayed the stubborn prayer of untested optimism, pleading desperately for God to heal David miraculously. But even now, some years later, I am not sure I ever really believed that God would heal him.

God answered both our prayers. He heard a mother's honest plea and gave her strength that she never had before. It was a quality of patient endurance, tinged with hope, that has grown year after year and never ceases to amaze this companion who knows her best. The strength she received has not failed her through other trials. It is not irony to say that God has produced in her a toughness of spirit and a gentleness of heart that can hardly be self-willed by anyone.

My own prayer God answered by saying no. I thought at first it was a harsh, uncaring no. When it became obvious David would die, I walked up to the fountain of bitterness, took the cup in my hands, and lifted it to my lips. I saw no reason not to drink it.

There seemed no sense in it at all. If God was love, if he really was omnipotent, then why would he let our precious little boy die? Three years old, bright-eyed, intelligent, he was full of energy. Life was just beginning. He had done no wrong, so why should he suffer such pain and death? Why? My brain burned with the question. Why?

# 9

# The Kind Professor Playing with David

*The only right way to read the Bible
is to learn how great and good God is,
to feel one's narrowness judged
and one's lack of faith,
and to accept day by day
larger loyalties and aims.*

- Nels F. S. Ferre

*I will turn their mourning into gladness; I will give them comfort and joy instead of sorrow. -- Jeremiah 31:13*

**DURING THE LAST SIX MONTHS OF DAVID'S LIFE I CONTINUED MY STUDIES IN THE VANDERBILT DIVINITY SCHOOL.** One of my subjects was "Systematic Theology," taught by Nels F. S. Ferre. Nobody ever struggled more desperately to understand the system, to see how the suffering of the innocent could fit into a system that defined God as love. The idea that "God is love" made no sense to me if at the same time God would let little children suffer and die.

My struggle was compounded by a negative attitude toward Doctor Ferre. I had been born in the Bible Belt, nurtured by Bible-believing Methodists and called to preach under the influence of solidly conservative preachers. Whether I was taught it or just caught it I quite early became suspicious of so-called liberal preachers and theologians. I presumed that disliking liberals was necessary to maintain my conservative image. Ferre was a liberal, so before I ever saw him, I disliked him. Since I was hurting emotionally because of David's suffering, I am sure this pain intensified my dislike.

Ferre insisted that his students get a grasp of his theology. To do this we had to read all of his more than a dozen books and report on each one. In my reviews I took special pains to blister Ferre with my perceptive insights into his gross theological errors, his radical departure from New Testament faith, and his lackadaisical ivory tower style.

In my report on one of his books I wrote, "Reading this book I get the impression that the author wrote this while sipping lemonade under a shade tree since his observations have little relevance for hurting people in the real world." (Years later I was profoundly ashamed that I had expressed such harsh words to so devout a servant of God. In ignorance I made fun of Ferre only to learn later that he had lost a child and that he himself had suffered from the crippling pain of rheumatoid arthritis. I was a brash and foolish young man yet thought I was a true Christian and Ferre a phony. My foolishness still embarrasses me!)

The good doctor's reaction surprised and aggravated me. He made no response to my hypercritical reports and consistently gave me high grades. His attitude toward me personally was equally unexpected. He was gracious, kind and obviously concerned for me, David and his mother. While I thought his theology quite unorthodox, I was forced to face the uncomfortable fact that his spirit had all the earmarks of a deeply authentic Christian.

The clinching evidence came when one day he called on us and sat on the floor to play with David in our dingy, rented house. It was while he was sitting on the floor playing with a sick child, not expecting anything in return for his kindness that I began to realize what a big man he was. I can still see that handsome Swede, his smile a mile wide, sprawled on that linoleum floor sharing the love of God with our dying boy. We were so wrapped up in our own pain that it never occurred to us that Ferre was also hurting. We know now that it had to be painful for a man with rheumatoid arthritis to sit down on the floor and play with a little boy. I can see them now: Ferre stacking several alphabet blocks and David knocking them over. David laughed and laughed as Ferre pretended to be upset while stacking the blocks again.

Since that afternoon I have had very little concern about whether a man is a liberal or a conservative. I saw "through a tear" that the only thing that really matters is whether Christ is in the heart. And Christ had filled the heart of Nels Ferre. The central focus of his theology was the agape love of God – the kind of love he personified in my presence during the last month of our son's life. More than any man I have known Nels Ferre helped liberate me from my narrow-minded conservatism. He did it by ignoring my reprehensible behavior and offering me his unconditional love. In doing so he introduced me to the God who suffers.

Other people called on us in those agonizing days of waiting. They all tried to help though the comfort of some pushed me closer to the cup of bitterness. More than one person counseled us to accept David's plight as the will of God. Inwardly I thought to myself, "If God is like that, I could hate him."

One woman, sincere but misinformed, suggested that we should be pleased that God was taking David for he probably needed another little boy for the Angelic Choir. I thought to myself, "I could hate a God like that." I pitied the woman's ignorance; people, even babies, do not become angels when they die.

Two weeks before David died his doctor advised us not to bring David back to the hospital. "There is nothing more we can do for him now," he said; "there is no need to put him through additional pain." Those words were his way of telling us that the end was near.

The end came early in the morning of a Thursday in the middle of May. For several days we had taken turns sitting in our rocking chair and holding his pain-ridden body in our arms. He had gotten too weak to struggle; his struggling was over. We kept giving him his medicine, thinking it would ease his pain some.

# 10

# Drinking Joy from Deathless Springs

*If He has put you in the shadow,
dwell there in order to bear witness
to the power of light to overcome it.
If you face failure and death,
testify through both
to God's total victory.*

- Nels F. S. Ferre

*When Jesus saw her weeping, and the Jews who had come along with her also weeping, he was deeply moved in spirit and troubled. "Where have you laid him? he asked. "Come and see, Lord," they replied. Jesus wept. -- John 11:33-35*

**During David's last night on earth neither of us slept much.** Dean rocked him until she was exhausted and I would take over. We were so tired we could hardly see straight. But we kept going. I thought I was the stronger one but Dean's perseverance amazed and humbled me. I saw firsthand the amazing power of a mother's love.

Dean had struggled out of bed and was walking into the room with David's medicine when the little fellow breathed his last breath. "It is time for his medicine," she said. I looked up at her, still holding his lifeless body in my arms, and said in tears, "Honey, he won't need his medicine anymore. He's gone. He is with Jesus now."

She helped me put his body down on the bed. We knelt down beside him, with our hands on his body, not saying a word. I wanted to pray but I did not know how. Numb and sobbing I felt one of Dean's hands gently patting me on my arm. Looking at the clock we realized David had died about five o'clock, just as the first rays of sunlight were breaking through the darkness.

One of our rituals during David's suffering was to play a 33 1/3 record that included two magnificent compositions by Johann Sebastian Bach – "Sheep May Safely Graze" and "Jesu, Joy of Man's Desiring." Night after night that music was like the Balm of Gilead helping us cling to our faith as we cried out to God for mercy. I can close my eyes and still hear the healing strains of that remarkable music. Looking back, I realized that though we were not aware of it then, we were through Bach's music "drinking joy from deathless springs."

After David's death we did not play that record for many years. It was too painful. On the simple headstone where David is buried we had inscribed an outline of a lamb and underneath it the words, "Jesus Loves Me.' Perhaps the haunting music of Bach's sheep safely grazing inspired us to put the lamb under David's name. I know that hearing either of those songs takes us back to David's nights of suffering and the way God used that music to soothe our broken hearts.

Nels Ferre had still another surprise in store for us. As soon as David died I called my close friend Jim Sellers. We had agreed that when I called him, he would notify the undertaker to come to our home. Jim did that but without my knowing it, he also called Doctor Ferre. To our utter amazement Ferre was at our front door two hours after David died! He was there long before the undertaker arrived.

Not only that, he was cheerful and smiling, almost radiant. In the bedroom Ferre startled us by lifting David's lifeless body off the bed. To our amazement he lifted David up as though he were offering him to God, which he did while praying aloud. Gently laying David's body back on the bed, he led us into our kitchen. There he sat down at our breakfast table between Dean and me.

I have long ago forgotten most of what he said, except one thing that is burned into my memory. With one arm around Dean and the other around me, hugging us close, he smiled and said, "I know how much your hearts hurt this morning. I just wanted to come and tell you that God hurts just like you hurt right now." The thought leaped into my mind, "I can love a God like that."

In the days and years that followed Ferre's words have reverberated in my soul again and again: "God hurts like you hurt." I began to believe that about God. It became the banner of love over my life. It has been the bedrock of my faith. I have shared it with thousands of people and I remain convinced that in these words we see the heart of God: He hurts like we hurt because he loves us and wants to take us in his arms as Nels Ferre took us in his arms on that awful May morning. There are many things I do not understand. But this much I know: On the day that David died the God who created heaven and earth met us in the hallways of hell and showed us the way out.

Now, looking back, I really do not understand why I did not drink at the fountain of bitterness. But it could be that while I was standing there, holding the cup, ready to drink, God sent a man who loved me and gently led me away, lifting to my parched lips a cup of the cool water of faith and hope. I know now that what could have been a day of overwhelming sadness became, in spite of our tears, the most important of those 233 days.  ✢

# *11*

## Days Of Mourning

*And so it is in our sadness that we discover a new aspect of God's character and reach a new understanding of Him that we could not have known without loss. He is acquainted with grief. He understands. He's not trying to rush us through our sadness. He's sad with us."*

- Nancy Guthrie

*"Weeping may remain for a night, but rejoicing comes in the morning." – Psalms 30:5*

**AFTER DAVID DIED WE BURIED HIS BODY IN THE OLD CEMETERY IN OUR HOMETOWN, WETUMPKA, ALABAMA.** The 233 days were history. Though death seems unbearable, life goes on. Days of mourning became the next chapter in our lives. During those days we struggled with depression, despair and self-pity.

We struggled with issues not covered in the grief handbooks. What should we do with David's toys now that he was gone? The sight of his toys was disturbing, especially the rocking horse he received at his last Christmas but was too weak to ride. We finally stored it, and other toys, in the attic of my parents' home. Out of sight, out of mind.

During David's suffering Dean had become rather stoic, internalizing her pain. She put on a brave front. She shed few tears. But her refusal to cry, we discovered, was a serious mistake. A few months after David's burial, Dean sat, trembling and frightened, in the office of Dr. Winston Edwards. The good doctor, known for his bluntness, said to her, "There is nothing wrong with you physically; your problem is emotional. What you need to do is have a good cry so the pain inside you can be released. You must learn to shed some tears if you want to stay alive!" A lot of tears stained Dean's cheeks for several days and she was soon well.

I had a similar problem with my grief, wanting everyone to think that I was strong and quite able to overcome my sorrow. But my brave front collapsed one day in Centennial Park while we were having a picnic lunch with our friend

Sister Maria. A nun whose friendship was a gift from God, Maria gently helped me release the boiling pain inside me. I did more than shed a few tears; I wept like a baby, sobbing uncontrollably for several minutes. In the days that followed my heart was filled with gratitude for the healing God provided that day for my wounded spirit.

Tears are necessary and helpful. In his kindness God made us so we can weep and find sweet release from our soul's burdens. Max Lucado offers a touching word about tears:

*"Tears. Those tiny drops of humanity. Those round, wet balls of fluid that tumble from our eyes, creep down our cheeks, and splash on the floor of our hearts. They were there that day. They are always present at such times. They should be; that's their job. They are miniature messengers; on call twenty-four hours a day to substitute for crippled words. They drip, drop and pour from the corner of our souls, carrying with them the deepest emotions we possess. They tumble down our faces with announcements that range from the most blissful joy to darkest despair. The principle is simple; when words are most empty, tears are most apt."*

Learning to weep without embarrassment proved to be a healthy decision for Dean and me. And our hearts say Amen to this observation by H. Norman Wright:

*"So much is distilled in our tears, not the least of which is wisdom in living life. From my own tears I have learned that if you follow your tears, you will find your heart. If you find your heart, you will find what is dear to God. And if you find what is dear to God, you will find the answer to how you should live your life."*

During the long days of mourning after losing David, we endured the disturbing thought that we might not have another child. We had loved being parents. We wanted a family and the possibility of not having other children was distressing. Later we would have to admit that we burdened ourselves with unnecessary worry for during the next eight years Dean gave birth to four more sons.

We were now graduate students in the School of Suffering. In the early stages of our grief we were frustrated by having people ask, "How long did it take you to get over David's death?" Over it? You don't get over the death of a loved one. But you can get "beyond" it and find healing for your broken heart.

So we did not struggle to "get over" David's death but to get beyond it. How we did that may be useful in your own journey with grief. What helped us were two big ideas: 1) recall, write down and retell memories of significant events; and 2) work together to develop winning attitudes about life.

I searched my memory bank, for example, for the details of that strange day when David was born. I recalled that dark clouds filled the sky. Light rain was falling. My wife and I were uneasy; we had heard the forecast of bad weather. But staying home was not an option. Dean's water had broken. She was enduring sharp and rapid labor pains. We had to get to the hospital. Our first child was about to discover America!

Though the stormy weather grew worse, we made it to the hospital in time. Dean was quickly in the hands of caring nurses. As was the custom in those days I was directed to the waiting room. Fathers were not allowed to witness the delivery of their child. I waited impatiently for several hours, unaware that a violent tornado had wreaked destruction across a wide path in the Auburn – Opelika area of central Alabama. By the time David Walter was born, the tornado had done its worst and moved on.

While Dean was birthing David the storm brought down nearby power lines, forcing the hospital to switch to emergency power. Torrents of rain rattled the hospital windows. Water poured into the hospital through the air-conditioning ducts.

Dr. Ben Thomas, our physician, had to drive through heavy rain to get to the small hospital that would become the thriving East Alabama Medical Center. Had he not arrived when he did, we would have been without his service. Shortly after his arrival, debris from the storm made driving in the area quite hazardous.

In the years that followed April 18 became more than just another day on the calendar. For Dean and me it has been that special day when our first son was born. We have celebrated it in many different ways.

One year recently we drove to the cemetery, stood by David's grave and holding hands, offered a prayer. We thanked God for the joy of having David with us for three brief years. We thanked God for what he taught us through David's suffering and for healing our grief-stricken hearts.

When David was born we were living in a small rented house at 818 Lakeview Drive in Auburn. The rent was $75 a month. I was in my third year at API, the land-grant college now known as Auburn University.

When I returned to the house, elated by the safe delivery of our firstborn, I found that the tornado had paid us a visit. The roof had been ripped off above the front door and rain had poured in, soaking some of our stuff. But our damage was incidental compared to the destruction of several homes nearby.

David was beautiful and healthy. His blond hair and blue eyes made him even more special. We were thrilled to have started our family. Though we had little money, we enjoyed life. The future was bright. We had the world by the tail. The next year I finished at Auburn and we moved to Nashville where I enrolled in the divinity school at Vanderbilt University.

Ten months later another storm descended upon us as swiftly as the tornado had come. Tests brought bad news about David. His voice breaking as he fought back tears, the kind doctor said, "Your son has leukemia."

You are no doubt aware that I am repeating details that I shared in previous chapters of this book. Let me explain why. It helps me, and it will help you in your journey with grief, to recall and retell what happened on significant days in our life journey. I invite you to do that – write out what you remember so you can think about it and find ways to share your story with family members and friends. Now let me go on.

As we sat there in shock, the doctor explained that there was no known cure. The best he could do would be to keep David comfortable until he died. "Perhaps," he said, "a cure will be discovered soon." (As you may know, years later medical research did provide a cure for many forms of leukemia, and in that we rejoice.)

I asked how long David had to live. His answer sent a

chill up and down my spine. "My best guess is somewhere between two months and two years," he said. It was the worst moment of my life – hearing that death sentence for our precious little boy.

The diagnosis shattered our world on that September day. David suffered. We struggled with the burden. We prayed. We cried. We stifled our anger, wrestled with our fear. We pled with God to heal David but to no avail. We watched helplessly as the disease slowly ravaged his body. Though he could run and play in the fall, by Christmas he could hardly walk. During his last three months he could not walk at all.

David's suffering finally ended in May the next year. His death wounded us but it did not destroy us. Though tested sorely by the loss of our only child, our marriage lasted and became stronger. God met us in the hallways of hell and showed us the way out. We refused to become bitter and let God make us better. Somehow, without really knowing what we were doing, we let God use our pain to help us overcome our grief. That is a lesson many of us have learned and a lesson all fellow strugglers should share with others. <u>God can use our pain to help us work through the grief process</u>.

Sadness, in the years that followed, gradually gave way to the overwhelming joy that is God's gift to those who keep holding his hand through tough times. So each year, on the 18th of April, Dean and I pause to give thanks that we are still together, still able to remember David's beautiful smile, and still thankful for the joy that was ours on the day our first child was born.

# *12*

## Embracing Winning Attitudes

*On the authority of Christ, there is not the slightest doubt but that we will see and know and love each other again…. The important thing for us to know is that there is another life which is within the reach of every one of us.*

- Charles L. Allen

*Jesus said to her, "I am the resurrection and the life. He who believes in me will live, even though he dies; and whoever lives and believes in me will never die." – John 11:25-26*

**EACH YEAR, AS THE MUGGY DAYS OF SEPTEMBER GIVE WAY** to the cooler days of October, Dean and I remember that awful September day when we learned our son was going to die. But we remember something far more important – that we were not alone during David's suffering or during our grieving journey. The living Christ was with us. He made his presence known. He graciously guided us to embrace winning attitudes that helped us make our way through the grief process.

We were 23 years old, too young to comprehend fully what it meant when the doctor said, "Your son is suffering from acute lymphoblastic leukemia and he has two months to two years to live. There is no cure. All we can do is make him as comfortable as possible until the end." While we were devastated by his words, our response to that report would influence the rest of our lives.

Looking back, it is difficult to understand why we did not drink at the fountain of bitterness. We felt forsaken by the God we had presumed loved us. We were seething with anger, bewilderment and disappointment. But it was while we held the bitter cup to our lips ready to drink that God sent a man to tenderly embrace us and gently lead us in another direction. Though we hardly recognized it at the time, we soon realized that God was guiding us into a winning perspective.

Within hours after David died, Dr. Nels F. S. Ferre, one of my Vanderbilt seminary professors, came to our home, to our great surprise. It was like God walking into our sorrow. He put his loving arms around us and said, "I know how much your hearts hurt. I just want to tell you that God hurts just like you hurt right now." Those words literally saved us from a life of bitterness. We both had the same response: I can love and trust a God like that!

Early on we were wrapped up in our grief. But gradually our lives changed when we realized that we were not the only people who endured loss and heartaches. God opened our eyes and our hearts to see the pain that others were experiencing. We began to learn that caring for hurting people is a medicine God uses to relieve the pain in our own hearts. Slowly we worked our way out of self-pity and found the strength to reach out to hurting people, people we could take in our own arms and remind them that God was hurting like they were hurting.

Today we can testify that God has remained just as trustworthy as He was when He saw us through our son's death. Folks our age talk about being in the sunset days of their lives but we like to think that we are moving toward a glorious sunrise. After all it was God's light that penetrated our darkness and rescued us from our grief.

The more we see those who are hurting, the more we want to share how good God is and how ready He is to walk with us through the valley of the shadow of death and give us the joy that comes in the morning. Without believing that He "hurt like we were hurting," we could never have walked through those dark days. And we cannot thank Him enough for the grace and guidance He has provided since we lost our David.

The Apostle Paul, great missionary of the first century, spent a good bit of time in jail. Then after several missionary journeys planting churches, he spent his last days in a jail in Rome. There it is believed he was executed by the Roman authorities. Had they been asked, Paul's Christian friends would have said that Paul was a prisoner of Caesar.

Paul's perspective was different. In his letter to the Ephesians Paul said, "I am a prisoner of Christ Jesus because of my preaching to you Gentiles." In his mind Paul was not a prisoner of Caesar; he was a prisoner of Jesus who was using his imprisonment to advance the gospel.

Your point of view makes a huge difference. How you see what is happening to you matters greatly. Take suffering for example. A friend lost her husband after a year of heartrending suffering. Not once did I hear her complain about God allowing this to happen to her husband. Instead she quietly explained to me how God had used her husband's suffering to strengthen her faith and the faith of her children.

How do you explain bad things happening to good people? Our viewpoints can differ widely. One person may believe that God does not have the power to prevent the suffering of the innocent. Another person may believe that God allows such suffering for reasons that remain a mystery to us. Your point of view makes a big difference because it determines how you feel about God.

Are the events of our lives happenchance or is there a plan being orchestrated by God? If I lose my job, I can moan and groan about how I was mistreated and make myself miserable. Or I can believe that God has a better plan for me and begin looking for doors that God will open for me. Your perspective matters; it determines your state of mind.

Perhaps the most well-known statement by the Apostle Paul is found in his Letter to the Romans, verse 8:28: *"And we know that in all things God works for the good of those who love him, who have been called according to his purpose."*

Can you believe that about God – that "in all things" He is working for your good? Even when you do not understand why certain things are happening? If you can, then you have a winning attitude! And that will make a profound difference in how you handle grief, even when mysteries cloud your mind.

You may view things differently. You are free to choose another point of view. But one thing seems clear: your perspective determines whether your mind is filled with peace and hope or dogged by fear and hopelessness. Is it not wise then to ask a loving God to help you choose daily perspectives that are healthy and hopeful? Surely it is!

In the movie, *The Shack*, the grieving father is following "God" up a winding trail in the woods. He becomes agitated and demands to know "Where are we going?" Patiently "God" replies, "Don't worry about that; just enjoy the journey, enjoy the journey."

That is good advice. Frantically rushing here and there, we can allow a maddening pace to rob us of the simple pleasures of this journey called life. Two weeks of isolation caused by a contagious illness gave me the opportunity to slow down and smell the roses.

Slow down. Enjoy the journey. Smell the roses. To do so is so important that I decided to make a note on my calendar, twice a month, to "smell the roses." The wisdom of doing this came to me when a good friend wrote recently, "Your isolation allowed you to stop the daily routine and take time to smell the roses. It is raining here this morning and I am using the time to smell some roses."

Ponder what it means for you to smell the roses. For me it means to focus on simple things, small pleasures that lower my blood pressure and remind me how blessed I am.

It calms my soul to sit quietly on our front porch and watch a humming bird flitting about, sipping quickly from the feeder. I speak to busy little bird: You need to slow down and smell some roses. A lovely bluebird gets my attention as he makes his way into his bird house. Nearby a squirrel is eyeing the bird feeder but awaiting my departure before going for some seed. In the distance the orange colors of the setting sun disappear in the darkening sky. Smelling roses – what a difference it makes!

The daily avalanche of "bargains" floods my cell phone and mailbox. Most I dump in the trash. Now and then one reminds me of roses. A Christian book advertisement read, "What's better than the smell of fresh flowers, the warm sunshine on your face, grass under your feet?" I did not order the book. Instead, while rain was gently falling, I walked to the mailbox in my bare feet, feeling the grass under my tender feet and smiling as raindrops clouded my glasses. I was smelling roses.

An email message slowed me down. A friend shared that the story of my isolation had touched her heart. She wrote, "I am now on hospice care for cancer but God is good even in this. I have had very little pain. The doctor says I have only a few months to live but God knows the timing and I am at peace. I covet your prayers and I will pray for you." I said a prayer for her. I was smelling roses.

My son who is a pastor called and shared with joy what a great Sunday he had enjoyed in his church. No comment about the attendance or the offering but his joy that a woman at the dry cleaners had come to church with her daughter. He had invited her several times and she finally came – and said she would come back! I gave thanks for the honor of having a son who delights in helping people connect with Jesus! I was smelling roses.

My wife loves a good bargain. Her face beaming, she showed me a little side table she had bought at the Adullam House for two dollars. And a lovely blouse she had purchased for four dollars. I applauded her frugality and thanked God for a partner who was not a spendthrift. I was smelling roses.

Our son the forester called and said, "Dad, let's buy some Red Oak lumber and build that table top you have been wanting to build for Mom." We bought some rough lumber from my friend Randy and planed it. The beauty of the wood was stunning. Mom was delighted with her new table. I was smelling roses.

You make the burden of grief easier to carry when you choose to slow down, smell the roses and enjoy the journey. After all, even though someone you loved is no longer with you, you are alive. And being alive you can make liberating choices that will lighten the load of your sorrow.

Choosing to think of problems as opportunities was a course correction that helped me immensely. When problems arise we are tempted to feel sorry for ourselves. Self-pity can take over and make our problems even worse.

A better response is to ask, "How can I turn this problem into an opportunity to improve my life? People are often willing to help you tackle a tough job. But they are not inclined to share your pity party.

Obstacles are in every person's path. We may stumble over them but if we work patiently and intentionally, we can turn obstacles into stepping stones. It is just a matter of seeing a stumbling block as a stepping stone.

We all fail and we succeed only by getting up – again and again. Henry Ford called failure "simply the opportunity to begin again, this time more intelligently."

As a new pastor I helped an old man remove an old wooden cross from the church lawn. He misled me. He said the old cross was an eyesore. My wise associate told me I had made a mistake, that removing the cross would be unsettling to the people who had put it there. We secured a new wooden cross and planted it where the old one had been. My problem became an opportunity.

Winston Churchill said "The pessimist sees difficulty in every opportunity. The optimist sees the opportunity in every difficulty." He was right. The optimist will look for the opportunity in every problem. And you have a choice; you can choose to be optimistic.

Paul and Silas were beaten and thrown into a prison that was a stinking dungeon. Did Paul whine about his imprisonment? No, he saw it as an opportunity to tell the prison guards about his friend Jesus. The Bible says that at midnight Paul and Silas were singing! Imagine that! Singing instead of whining about their problems!

Singing helps us see problems as opportunities. One of my favorite songs is "Until Then." The words and the music were composed by Stuart Hamblen. I love the way he reminds us that heartaches can become stepping stones. Expect a blessing when you read Hamblen's song:

*My heart can sing when I pause to remember*
*A heartache here is but a stepping stone*
*Along a trail that's winding always upward,*
*This troubled world is not my final home.*

The chorus is my philosophy of life. I love it. I will sing it at the drop of a hat. Hamblen captures my heart when he says in the face of problems we should "carry on with joy" and keep on singing until the Lord calls us home.

Be careful when you read the chorus. You may break out singing and see your problem as an opportunity!

*But until then, my heart will go on singing,*
*Until then, with joy I'll carry on;*
*Until the day my eyes behold the city,*
*Until the day God calls me home.*

Losing my son was the most gut-wrenching problem I ever faced. But it was not the end of the world. Life went on and somehow I found the strength to go on with it. My recovery began with the breathtaking idea that God hurt like I was hurting. Then I found I was not alone. Christ was with me. With his strengthening presence I had hope for the future.

Whenever I was about to give up and wallow in self-pity, Christ said, "Walter, get up and go again; I will help you pick up the pieces. I am going to use your pain to make you a better person. I will help you find joy in serving other hurting people, offering them the comfort I have given you. If you want to be my servant, that is how you do it. So come on. I will walk with you so you will have no fear on this dark pathway. Together we will walk out of this heartbreaking bewilderment into the light of my glory. One day you will hold David in your arms again, but untll then, until that day, I will give you the joy to carry on."

With weak knees and trembling hands, I took His hand again and again and he turned my heartaches into stepping stones. Serving Him by loving hurting people has led me into incredible joy, the joy of knowing that the God who hurts like I hurt would be all I need for the long journey home.

Glory!

**Walter Albritton**, a United Methodist minister, lives with his wife Dean at The Cabin near Wetumpka, Alabama.

**Further Reading from the Quoted Text**

**Charles L. Allen** – *When You Lose a Loved One*, Fleming H. Revell Company, 1959

**Kennon L. Callahan** -- *Twelve Keys for Living: Possibilities for a Whole, Healthy Life*, Jossey-Bass, 1998

**John Claypool** -- *Stages*, Word Books, 1977

**Nels F. S. Ferre** -- *Strengthening the Spiritual Life*, Harper & Brothers, 1951

**Nancy Guthrie** – *Holding on to Hope*, Tyndale House, Wheaton, Ill., 2002

**Ben Campbell Johnson** -- *Discerning God's Will*, Westminster/John Knox Press, 1990

**Max Lucado** – *No Wonder They Call Him the Savior*, Multnomah Press, 1986

**Elton Trueblood** -- *The Common Ventures of Life: Birth, Work, Death*, Harper Row, 1949

**Dallas Willard** – *Renovation of the Heart*, NAVPRESS, 2002

**H. Norman Wright** – *Experiencing Grief*, B&H Publishing Group, Nashville, TN, 2004

Made in the USA
Lexington, KY
23 December 2017